WOLFGANG AMADEUS MOZART

CLARINET CONCERTO

A major/A-Dur/La majeur
K 622

Edited by
Richard Clarke

Ernst Eulenburg Ltd

London · Mainz · Madrid · New York · Paris · Prague · Tokyo · Toronto · Zürich

CONTENTS

The present edition of Mozart's Clarinet Concerto, K622, is based on readings of the relevant texts published in *Wolfgang Amadeus Mozart: Neue Ausgabe sämtlicher Werke*, V/14.2

© 2009 Ernst Eulenburg & Co GmbH, Mainz
for Europe excluding the British Isles
Ernst Eulenburg Ltd, London
for all other countries

Ernst Eulenburg Ltd
48 Great Marlborough Street
London W1F 7BB

PREFACE

The Clarinet Concerto is the last major work Mozart lived to complete. His next project was the D minor *Requiem*, left unfinished at his death on 5 December 1791. In a letter to his wife Constanze, written between 7 and 8 October of that last year, Mozart mentions that he has just 'orchestrated almost the whole Rondò' of the Concerto, which would suggest that by this stage the work was substantially complete. Many commentators have marvelled at the speed with which Mozart appears to have composed the Concerto: evidence suggests that most of the work was done during the first week of October. However, he was not working from scratch. At some stage, possibly a year or two earlier, Mozart had begun a Concerto in G major for basset horn (despite its name, this is actually the tenor instrument of the clarinet family). The detailed draft score extends to 199 bars and is very close in substance to the first movement orchestral and solo expositions plus the beginning of the development of K622.

It was not unusual for Mozart to sketch out the beginning of a work and then put it to one side, taking it up some time later when an opportunity for performance arose. The Piano Concerto in A major K488 for example, was begun 1784, with oboes instead of the now familiar clarinets. Mozart completed it in 1786, adjusting the orchestration to suit the forces available – any opportunity to use clarinets was welcomed by Mozart. In the case of the Clarinet Concerto the stimulus was a request from the great Viennese virtuoso Anton Stadler, who gave the first performance in Prague on 16 October, just over a week after the above-quoted letter to Constanze. Stadler was one of the musicians Mozart admired most warmly. The two men had met shortly after Mozart had arrived in Vienna in 1781. Stadler's reputation was already impressive: in that same year the Emperor had publicly described him as 'indispensable'. Stadler's phenomenal technical agility was matched by an expressive musicality which marked him out amongst his peers. A contemporary critic observed that 'one would never had thought that a clarinet could imitate the human voice to such perfection'.

Such playing would have appealed strongly to Mozart. As the fortepianist and Mozart authority Robert Levin aptly remarks, there are marked 'anthropomorphic' qualities to the solo writing in Mozart's concertos, inviting direct comparison with his operatic and concert arias. Both domains demonstrate Mozart's genius in character portrayal while reconciling virtuosity with the needs of dramatic expression; both deploy prodigious melodic invention, a fluid rhythmic language and a voluptuous orchestra fabric.[1]

In these respects Stadler's playing probably came closer to Mozart's ideals than anyone else's – except perhaps his own. Stadler took part in the premieres of a number of important Mozart works, in all of which he appears to have given special satisfaction to the composer. In 1784, the two men played together in the first performance of the Quintet for piano and winds K452, which the delighted Mozart then pronounced 'the best thing' he had written. Stadler's performance of the clarinet part may well have influenced that slightly surprising judgement – surprising because by this stage Mozart had already composed his magnificent Mass in C minor K427, and the first three of his six great 'Haydn' quartets, K387 in G major, K421 in D minor, and K428 in E flat major, widely counted amongst his finest achievements, and all of them more ambitious technically and in 'character portrayal' than the Quintet.

So it is easy to understand how the chronically overworked Mozart might still have leapt at the opportunity to rework and complete his earlier basset-horn concerto draft for Stadler in October 1791. The result was more or less the

[1] 'Concertos', in *The Mozart Compendium*, ed. H. C. Robbins Landon (London, 1990), 263

IV

Clarinet Concerto as we know it today, though with one significant difference. The instrument Stadler played – and indeed had personally devised – had a slightly deeper range than the modern clarinet in A, taking it down to a written low C (concert A). Though Stadler had great success with the instrument, it soon fell out of favour (no examples of Stadler's deeper A clarinet have survived), to be replaced by the familiar clarinets in A and B flat. The version of the score that has been familiar for the best part of two centuries is a reworking for the modern clarinet in A with some of the deeper bass notes transposed. Almost certainly this arrangement was not made by Mozart himself. In March 1802, a review of the first edition of the parts of the Clarinet Concerto, as published by Breitkopf & Härtel, appeared in the *Allgemeine Musikalische Zeitung*. Here the unnamed critic – while praising the music generally – complains about the new version of the solo part, comparing it unfavourably with what he claims to have heard Stadler play.

Whereas currently such clarinets descending to low C can still be counted among the rare instruments, one is indebted to the editors, who spared no pains in making these transpositions and alterations for the normal clarinet, although the concerto has not exactly gained thereby. It might have been better to have published it entirely according to the original, and to have rendered the transpositions and alterations at most by small notes

Tradition has a way of sanctioning all manner of oddities and anomalies in works of art, so it is perhaps unsurprising that critics in later generations were not inclined to find fault with the reworked clarinet part in the familiar edition of K622 – until, that is, the rise of the 'period instrument' movement in the 1980s inevitably brought the issue to the fore again. Alas, Mozart's original manuscript had long disappeared, and with it any part material used by Stadler for the 1791 first performance. Constanze Mozart had no doubt at all where the blame lay, accusing Stadler of pawning it – along with several other Mozart manuscripts – for an unimpressive 73 ducats. However the sketch score for the G

major basset-horn concerto has survived, and it gives several crucial clues as to how the original solo part might have differed from the version hallowed by tradition. Take the figure in bars 94-5 of the first movement for example: when one knows that the clarinet Mozart wrote for could reach down to low written C, the awkwardness of the movement from the last three quavers of bar 94 to the semiquaver figures of bar 95 virtually leaps off the page. Even without the evidence of the original basset-horn draft, a simple analogy with bars 96-7 would be enough to indicate what Mozart's original intentions must surely have been. It is hard to believe that Mozart – even under extreme pressure – would have settled for a crude part-transposition like the one perpetuated since the first edition. Another striking example comes at the climax of the *Adagio* (bars 55ff.). Given an instrument like Stadler's, with an extra major third in the bass register, there would have been no need to break up the demisemiquaver arpeggios on the second beats of bars 55 and 57. A continuous upward movement starting on low C is more elegant, and it allows the soloist to demonstrate a far wider range of tone colour at this dramatic high point of the movement.

Since interest in the nature of the original Clarinet Concerto began to re-awaken in recent times, attempts have been made to reconstruct the solo part as Mozart might have intended it, and clarinets have been built with the same extended bass compass as Stadler's instrument. The result has been christened the 'basset clarinet', and has become increasingly popular in both the concert hall and the recording studio: so much so that it now enjoys almost equal popularity with the modern A clarinet. However, there is no sign that the latter instrument is in serious decline in performances of K622.

Rightly or wrongly, the fact that the Clarinet Concerto is Mozart's last completed major work has inevitably affected the way it has been performed and discussed. The scholar H. C. Robbins Landon was clearly not expecting any serious disagreement when he wrote, in the mid

1950s, that 'no other work by Mozart is more imbued with that final, quiet resignation [...] The concerto is Mozart's farewell to the realms of pure music'.[2] Robbins Landon goes on to state that 'by October [Mozart] must have guessed the extent of his illness', but there is no solid evidence to support that hypothesis, or that he had any serious intuition that he was nearing the end of his life. By the time Robbins Landon returned to the subject three decades later in his important study *1791: Mozart's Last Year*, he had revised his opinion substantially, arguing instead that Mozart was on the brink of a 'new era',[3] buoyed up by the recent huge success of his opera *Die Zauberflöte* K620, and looking forward eagerly to his promised appointment as Kapellmeister at St Stephen's Cathedral, Vienna, on the death or retirement of the then incumbent, Leopold Hofmann. Certainly there are parts in the Clarinet Concerto – particularly in the central *Adagio* – which show a distinctly melancholy cast of expression. Interestingly, performance on the basset clarinet, with the solo range extended downwards accordingly, does tend to bring a more sombre colouring to other passages. However it would be just as easy to identify a 'final, quiet resignation' in the slow movement and finale introduction of the String Quintet in G minor K516 written four years earlier. The emotional colouring of both these works may have more to do with a possible depressive tendency in Mozart's character than with any alleged mystical intuition of approaching death in October 1791.

Nevertheless, the Clarinet Concerto's mythological status as Mozart's 'farewell to the realms of pure music' has proved enduring and influential. Perhaps the quasi-sacred aura associated with the work helps explain the puzzling fact that so few lastingly successful clarinet concertos have been composed since Mozart's death, despite the instrument's eminent suitability as a virtuoso soloist on the large concert stage. Undeniably the modern repertoire is significantly richer in chamber music featuring solo clarinet than in major clarinet concertos. Moreover the most successful works for clarinet and orchestra, from the concertos of Weber and Bernhard Henrik Crusell to Harrison Birtwistle's *Melencolia I*, rarely betray any signs of engaging with the Mozart Concerto as a model. A possible exception is the opening movement of Aaron Copland's Clarinet Concerto (1947-8), whose sweetly nostalgic tone and lyrical use of wide intervallic leaps could be said to show Mozart's influence. A more specific invocation however can be found towards the end of the one-movement Clarinet Concerto by Carl Nielsen (1928), written at a time when its composer was haunted by thoughts of his own mortality. At Fig. 41 (*Poco adagio*) in the Nielsen Concerto the clarinet (also in A) plays a melodic idea centred on the same two notes (concert G and C) with which the solo exposition of the Mozart Concerto begins – an idea which could with more justification be said to express 'final, quiet resignation' than anything in K622. If this is a direct tribute to Mozart's Clarinet Concerto, perhaps its very nature – an offering from one composer nearing death to another – explains why such acts of homage have been relatively rare.

Stephen Johnson

[2] 'The Concertos (2)' in *The Mozart Companion*, ed. H. C. Robbins Landon & Donald Mitchell (London, 1956), 279
[3] H. C. Robbins Landon *1791: Mozart's Last Year* (London, 1988), 147

VORWORT

Das Klarinettenkonzert ist das letzte große Werk, das Mozart fertig stellte; sein nächstes, das *Requiem* in d-Moll, blieb durch seinen Tod am 5. Dezember 1791 unvollendet. In einem Brief an seine Frau Konstanze, geschrieben zwischen dem 7. und 8. Oktober desselben Jahres, erwähnt Mozart „Instrumentierte ich fast das ganze Rondò". Es ist daher anzunehmen, dass zu dieser Zeit das Konzert praktisch fertig war. Viele Kommentatoren staunten über die Geschwindigkeit, mit der Mozart das Konzert offenbar komponierte: Alles deutet darauf hin, dass der Großteil der Arbeit in der ersten Oktoberwoche fertig war. Allerdings musste er nicht bei Null anfangen. Einige Zeit zuvor, möglicherweise ein oder zwei Jahre, hatte er ein Konzert in G-Dur für Bassetthorn begonnen (trotz des Namens ist dies das Tenorinstrument der Klarinettenfamilie). Der detaillierte Partiturentwurf umfasst 199 Takte und ähnelt vom musikalischen Material dem ersten Satz von KV 622 bezüglich der Orchester- und Soloexpositionen sowie dem Anfang der Durchführung.

Es war nicht ungewöhnlich, dass Mozart den Anfang eines Werkes entwarf, um es dann beiseite zu legen und später, wenn die Möglichkeit einer Aufführung bestand, wieder hervorzuholen. Als beispielsweise 1784 das Klavierkonzert in A-Dur KV 488 begonnen wurde, enthielt es Oboen an Stelle von Klarinetten. Mozart vollendete das Werk 1786 und passte die Instrumentierung den verfügbaren Instrumentalisten an – jede Gelegenheit zum Einsatz von Klarinetten war ihm willkommen. Die Anregung zum Klarinettenkonzert war eine Bitte des großen Wiener Virtuosen Anton Stadlers, der das Werk am 16. Oktober in Prag uraufführte, gerade eine Woche nach dem oben erwähnten Brief an Konstanze. Mozart bewunderte Stadler sehr. Die beiden hatten sich getroffen, kurz nachdem Mozart 1781 nach Wien gekommen war. Damals war Stadlers Ruf bereits beeindruckend: Im selben Jahr hatte der Kaiser ihn öffentlich als „unentbehrlich" bezeichnet. Stadlers phänomenale Technik war mit einer ausdrucksstarken Musikalität gepaart, die ihn aus seinen Musikerkollegen hervorstechen ließ. Ein zeitgenössischer Rezensent schrieb: „Hätt's nicht gedacht, daß ein Klarinet menschliche Stimme so täuschend nachahmen könnte."

Mozart war für solches Spiel äußerst empfänglich. Wie Robert Levin, Fortepianist und Mozart-Autorität, treffend feststellte, gibt es markante „anthropomorphische" Qualitäten in den Solos von Mozarts Konzerten, die zu direkten Vergleichen mit seinen Opern- und Konzertarien einluden.

Beide Sphären zeigen Mozarts Genie als Charakterporträtist, indem er Virtuosität mit den Notwendigkeiten dramatischen Ausdrucks vereint; in beiden Fällen gibt es unglaubliche melodische Erfindungen, eine fließende, rhythmische Sprache und ein üppiges Orchestergefüge.[1]

Diesbezüglich kam Stadlers Spiel Mozarts Ideal vermutlich näher als demjenigen irgendeines anderen – außer vielleicht seinem eigenen. Stadler spielte in etlichen Premieren wichtiger Werke von Mozart, und immer dürfte es zu dessen äußerster Zufriedenheit gewesen sein. 1784 musizierte die beiden zusammen in der Uraufführung des Quintetts für Klavier und Bläser, KV 452, das den erfreuten Mozart zu der Bemerkung veranlasste, es wäre „das Beste", was er je geschrieben hat. Stadlers Ausführung der Klarinettenstimme könnte das etwas überraschende Urteil beeinflusst haben – überraschend deshalb, weil Mozart zu dieser Zeit schon seine herrliche Messe in c-Moll, KV 427, und die ersten drei seiner großen Haydn Quartette komponiert hatte: KV 387 in G-Dur, KV 421 in d-Moll und KV 428 in Es-Dur, die weithin zu seinen größten Errungenschaften zählen und technisch sowie in der „Charakterzeichnung" ambitionierter als das Quintett sind.

[1] „Concertos", in: *The Mozart Compendium*, Hg. H. C. Robbins Landon, London, 1990, S. 263.

Es ist daher leicht verständlich, dass der ständig überarbeitete Mozart auch diese Gelegenheit beim Schopf packte, den früheren Entwurf für das Bassetthorn-Konzert umzuarbeiten und im Oktober 1791 für Stadler fertig zu stellen. Das Resultat bestand mehr oder minder im Klarinettenkonzert, das wir heute kennen, doch mit einem bedeutenden Unterschied. Stadlers Klarinette – die er selbst entworfen hatte – reichte etwas tiefer als die moderne A-Klarinette: bis zum geschriebenen tiefen C (klingendes A). Obwohl Stadler großen Erfolg auf diesem Instrument hatte, kam es bald aus der Mode (kein Exemplar von Stadlers tieferer A-Klarinette ist erhalten) und wurde von den heute bekannten A- und B-Klarinetten abgelöst. Die seit zwei Jahrhunderten bekannte Partiturfassung ist eine Überarbeitung für die moderne A-Klarinette, die einige der tieferen Bassnoten transponiert. Höchstwahrscheinlich stammt diese Bearbeitung nicht von Mozart selbst. Im März 1802 erschien in der *Allgemeinen Musikalischen Zeitung* eine Rezension der ersten Ausgabe von Stimmen des Klarinettenkonzerts, publiziert von Breitkopf & Härtel. Obwohl anonyme Kritiker die Musik generell lobt, beschwert er sich über die neue Fassung der Solostimme, die er nachteilig mit dem Spiel Stadlers, den er angeblich gehört hatte, vergleicht.

Da es heutzutage nur wenige Klarinetten gibt, die bis zum tiefen C hinunter reichen, ist den Herausgebern zu danken, die keine Mühe scheuten, die Transponierungen und Veränderungen für eine normale Klarinette anzugeben, obwohl man nicht sagen kann, dass das Konzert hierdurch besser geworden wäre. Vielleicht wäre es besser gewesen, das Werk gänzlich dem Original folgend herauszugeben und die Transponierungen und Veränderungen allenfalls in kleinen Noten zu ergänzen.

Tradition kann jedwede Eigenheit und Anomalie in Kunstwerken zulassen. So ist es vielleicht wenig erstaunlich, dass spätere Kritiker nichts an der umgearbeiteten Klarinettenstimme in der vertrauten Ausgabe von KV 622 auszusetzen hatten – das heißt solange, bis das Aufkommen der „alte Instrumente"-Bewegung in den 1980er Jahren die Sache wieder in den Vordergrund rückte. Leider war Mozarts ursprüngliches Manuskript längst verschollen und mit ihm jedes Stimmenmaterial, das Stadler bei der ersten Aufführung 1791 benutzt hatte. Konstanze Mozart hatte keinen Zweifel, bei wem die Schuld lag, und beschuldigte Stadler, das Material – zusammen mit anderen Handschriften Mozarts – für schäbige 73 Dukaten verpfändet zu haben. Der Entwurf der Partitur zum Bassetthorn-Konzert in G-Dur hat allerdings überlebt und gibt uns einige entscheidende Hinweise, wie die ursprüngliche Solostimme sich von der traditions-geheiligten Fassung unterschieden haben mag. Als Beispiel möge die Figur in Takt 94–95 des ersten Satzes dienen: Wenn man weiß, dass die Klarinette, für die Mozart schrieb, das tiefe C erreichen konnte, springt die Unbeholfenheit der Bewegung von den letzten 3 Achteln in Takt 94 bis zur Sechzehntelfigur in Takt 95 sofort ins Auge. Aber auch ohne den Beweis des originalen Entwurfs für Bassetborn sollte ein einfacher Vergleich mit den Takten 96–97 ausreichen um zu zeigen, was Mozarts ursprüngliche Intention gewesen sein muss. Es ist kaum glaubhaft, dass er sich – sogar unter größtem Druck – mit einer derart groben Stimmtransposition zufrieden gegeben hätte, wie sie seit der ersten Ausgabe überliefert worden war. Ein weiteres eindrückliches Beispiel findet sich beim Höhepunkt des *Adagios* (Takt 55ff). Mit einem Instrument wie demjenigen Stadlers, das eine zusätzliche große Terz im Bassbereich hatte, bestände keine Notwendigkeit, die Zweiunddreißigstel-Arpeggios auf dem zweiten Schlag der Takte 55 und 57 zu teilen. Eine fortlaufende Aufwärtsbewegung beginnend auf dem tiefen C ist viel eleganter, und erlaubt dem Solisten ein viel breiteres Tonkolorit am dramatischen Höhepunkt des Satzes.

Nachdem in jüngster Zeit wieder neues Interesse am Wesen des ursprünglichen Klarinettenkonzerts zu erwachen begann, wurden auch Versuche unternommen, die Solostimme so, wie sie Mozart beabsichtigt haben könnte, zu rekonstruieren. Dafür wurden Klarinetten mit dem gleichen erweiterten Bassumfang wie bei Stadlers Instrument gebaut. Das Resultat war

VIII

die so genannte „Bassett-Klarinette", die in Konzertsaal und Tonstudio immer beliebter wird, und zwar derart, dass sie sich heute fast der gleichen Beliebtheit wie die A-Klarinette erfreut. Das heißt jedoch nicht, dass der Gebrauch der A-Klarinette bei Aufführungen von KV 622 merklich abnimmt.

Ob zu Recht oder zu Unrecht: Die Tatsache, dass das Klarinettenkonzert Mozarts letztes vollendetes Werk ist, hat die Art und Weise der Aufführung und Diskussion beeinflusst. Der Wissenschaftler H. C. Robbins Landon erwartete bestimmt keinen ernstlichen Widerspruch, als er Mitte der 1950er Jahre schrieb, dass „kein anderes Mozartwerk mehr von tiefer, stiller Resignation durchtränkt ist [...] Das Konzert ist Mozarts Abschied vom Reich der reinen Musik".[2] Robbins Landon führt aus, dass Mozart „im Oktober das Ausmaß seiner Krankheit geahnt haben musste", doch gibt es keinerlei soliden Beweis für diese These, oder dass er eine ernstliche Intuition von seinem bevorstehenden Tod gehabt hätte. Als Robbins Landon drei Jahrzehnte später dieses Thema in seiner wichtigen Untersuchung *1791: Mozarts Letztes Jahr* wieder aufgriff, hatte er seine Meinung wesentlich geändert und argumentierte stattdessen, dass Mozart am Beginn einer „neuen Ära"[3] gestanden habe, beflügelt vom jüngsten großen Erfolg seiner Oper *Die Zauberflöte*, KV 620, und in freudiger Erwartung der ihm versprochenen Stelle als Kapellmeister des Stephansdoms in Wien, sobald der Amtsinhaber Leopold Hofmann entweder in den Ruhestand treten oder sterben würde. Sicherlich gibt es Stellen im Klarinettenkonzert, die sehr melancholische Züge aufweisen – insbesondere im zentralen *Adagio*. Interessanterweise bringt das Spiel auf der Bassettklarinette mit dem in die Tiefe erweiterten Solobereich auch in anderen Passagen ein dunkleres Kolorit. Andererseits ließe sich ebenso gut eine „tiefe, stille Resignation" im langsamen Satz sowie der letzten Einleitung des vier Jahre früher komponierten Streichquintetts in G moll, KV 516, erken-

nen. Die emotionale Färbung dieser beiden Werke mag mehr mit einer möglichen depressiven Tendenz in Mozarts Charakter zusammenhängen als mit angeblich mystischer Intuition vom bevorstehenden Tod im Oktober 1791.

Jedenfalls erwies sich der mythologische Status des Klarinettenkonzerts als Mozarts „Abschied aus dem Reich der reinen Musik" als lang anhaltend und einflussreich. Möglicherweise kann die mit dem Werk verbundene quasi-geheiligte Aura den Umstand erklären, dass seit Mozarts Tod so wenige dauerhaft erfolgreiche Klarinettenkonzerte komponiert wurden, obwohl das Instrument als virtuoses Soloinstrument auf einer großen Konzertbühne bestens geeignet ist. Zweifellos ist das moderne Repertoire bedeutend reichhaltiger an Kammermusik mit Soloklarinette als an größeren Klarinettenkonzerten. Auch zeigen die erfolgreichsten Werke für Klarinette und Orchester – von den Konzerten Webers und Berhard Henrik Crusells bis hin zu Harrison Birtwistles *Melencolia I* – kaum Anzeichen, dass Mozarts Konzert ihr Vorbild gewesen wäre. Eine mögliche Ausnahme ist der erste Satz in Aaron Coplands Klarinettenkonzert (1947/48), dessen lieblich-nostalgischer Ton und lyrischer Gebrauch von weiten Intervallsprüngen Mozarts Einfluss zeigen mag. Ein deutlicherer Anklang findet sich gegen Ende des einsätzigen Klarinettenkonzerts von Carl Nielsen (1928), geschrieben, als der Komponist von Gedanken an seine eigene Sterblichkeit heimgesucht war. Bei Ziffer 41 (*Poco adagio*) von Nielsens Konzert spielt die Klarinette (ebenfalls in A) eine melodische Idee, die sich um die gleichen zwei Noten (klingendes G und C) bewegt, mit denen die Soloexposition von Mozarts Konzert beginnt – eine Idee, von der man eher als von KV 622 sagen könnte, sie drücke „tiefe, stille Resignation" aus. Falls hier Mozarts Klarinettenkonzert direkter Tribut gezollt wird, erklärt sich vielleicht aus der Natur der Sache – der Ehrung eines Komponisten am Rand des Todes an einen anderen –, warum solche Huldigungen ziemlich selten sind.

Stephen Johnson
Übersetzung: Burgi Hartmann

[2] „The Concertos (2)" in: *The Mozart Companion*, Hg. H. C. Robbins Landon & Donald Mitchell, London, 1956, S. 279.
[3] H. C. Robbins Landon: *1791: Mozart's Last Year*, London 1988, S. 147.

PRÉFACE

Le Concerto pour clarinette est la dernière œuvre achevée de Mozart, le *Requiem* en *ré* mineur qui le suivit ayant été interrompu à sa mort, le 5 décembre 1791. Dans une lettre écrite entre le 7 et le 8 octobre de cette dernière année, Mozart rapporte à son épouse Constance qu'il vient « d'orchestrer presque tout le *Rondo* » du Concerto, ce qui laisse à penser que l'œuvre était alors pratiquement terminée. Nombre de commentateurs se sont émerveillés de la rapidité avec laquelle Mozart semble avoir composé le Concerto, tant les faits suggèrent que l'essentiel de cette œuvre prit forme pendant la première semaine d'octobre. Toutefois, Mozart ne partait pas de rien. Environ une ou deux années auparavant, il avait commencé à écrire un Concerto en *sol* majeur pour cor de basset (qui, malgré son nom, est l'instrument ténor de la famille des clarinettes) dont l'ébauche détaillée de 199 mesures se révèle de substance très proche des expositions de l'orchestre et du soliste et du début du développement du K.622.

Il n'était pas inhabituel pour Mozart d'esquisser le début d'une œuvre, de la laisser de côté, puis de la reprendre plus tard quand une occasion de l'exécuter se présentait. Ainsi, par exemple, le Concerto pour piano en *la* majeur, K.488, fut-il commencé en 1784, avec des hautbois au lieu des désormais fameuses clarinettes, et achevé en 1786, Mozart arrangeant son orchestration en fonction des effectifs disponibles – toute opportunité de faire jouer des clarinettes fut pour lui la bienvenue. Dans le cas du Concerto pour clarinette, l'incitation vint de la demande formulée par le grand virtuose viennois Anton Stadler, qui le créa à Prague le 16 octobre, un peu plus d'une semaine après la lettre adressée à Constance citée plus haut. Stadler était l'un des musiciens que Mozart admirait le plus ardemment. La rencontre entre les deux hommes remontait à peu de temps après l'arrivée de Mozart à Vienne en 1781. Stadler y jouissait déjà d'une réputation im-

pressionnante : l'empereur l'avait, cette même année, qualifié publiquement d' « indispensable ». L'agilité technique phénoménale de Stadler s'alliait à une musicalité et une expression qui le singularisaient parmi ses pairs. Un critique contemporain s'exclama en l'entendant : « On n'aurait jamais imaginé qu'une clarinette pût imiter si parfaitement la voix humaine ».

De telles capacités d'interprète attirèrent fortement Mozart. Ainsi que l'a fait justement remarquer le fortepianiste et expert, Robert Levin, les qualités nettement « anthropomorphiques » rencontrées dans l'écriture des solos des concertos de Mozart les rapprochent directement de ses arias d'opéra et de concert :

Les deux genres montrent le génie de caractérisation des personnages de Mozart, réconciliant la virtuosité et les besoins de l'expression dramatique. Tous deux déploient une invention mélodique prodigieuse, un langage rythmique fluide et une orchestration voluptueuse.[1]

Sur ces aspects, le jeu de Stadler assimila probablement plus que tout autre l'idéal conçu par Mozart – à l'exception, peut-être de sa propre interprétation. Stadler participa à la création de nombreuses œuvres importantes de Mozart et combla, apparemment, à chaque fois le compositeur d'une satisfaction particulière. En 1784, les deux artistes créèrent ensemble le Quintette avec piano et instruments à vent, K.452, que Mozart déclara, enchanté, « la meilleure chose » qu'il ait écrite. L'interprétation de Stadler de la partie de clarinette a sûrement influencé ce jugement quelque peu surprenant, Mozart ayant, en effet, à cette époque déjà composé sa magnifique Messe en *ut* mineur, K.427, et les trois premiers de ses six grands quatuors « dédiés à Haydn », K.387 en *sol* majeur, K.421 en *ré* mineur et K.428 en *mi* bémol majeur, largement reconnus parmi ses plus belles œuvres et tous plus ambitieux, à la fois techniquement et par

[1] « Concertos » in : *The Mozart Compendium*, éd. H.C. Robbins Landon, Londres, 1990, p.263

leur « personnification », que le Quintette.

On comprend aisément que Mozart, en surmené chronique, ait encore saisi, en octobre 1791, l'occasion de retravailler et de terminer son ancienne ébauche de concerto pour cor de basset à l'intention de Stadler. Le Concerto pour clarinette qui en résulta est plus ou moins celui que nous connaissons aujourd'hui, avec toutefois une différence notoire. L'instrument joué par Stadler – qu'il avait conçu lui-même – possédait une tessiture légèrement plus grave que la clarinette moderne en *la*, descendant jusqu'au *do* noté (*la* réel). En dépit du succès de Stadler, cet instrument disparut bientôt (aucun exemplaire de la clarinette grave en *la* de Stadler n'a survécu) en faveur des clarinettes en *la* et en *si* bémol ultérieures. La version de cette partition diffusée depuis près de deux cents ans est un arrangement réalisé pour la clarinette moderne en *la* – certaines des notes les plus graves ayant été transposées – mais qui ne le fut certainement pas par Mozart lui-même. En mars 1802, un compte-rendu de la première édition des parties séparées du Concerto pour clarinette, publiée chez Breitkopf und Härtel, parut dans l'*Allgemeine Musikalische Zeitung*. Son signataire anonyme, quoique généralement élogieux pour la musique, déplore la nouvelle version de la partie de soliste, qu'il compare en sa défaveur à celle qu'il dit avoir entendu Stadler jouer :

Comme il n'existe aujourd'hui que peu d'instruments qui atteignent le *do* grave, on peut être reconnaissant aux éditeurs de ne s'être épargné aucune peine pour effectuer les transpositions et modifications nécessaires à une clarinette normale, bien qu'on ne puisse affirmer que le Concerto s'en soit trouvé amélioré. Peut-être aurait-il mieux valu éditer l'œuvre en suivant sa version originale et y ajouter les transpositions et modifications à l'aide de notes en petits caractères.

L'usage trouvant moyen de sanctionner toutes sortes de bizarreries et d'anomalies concernant les œuvres d'art, il n'est sans doute pas étonnant que les critiques des générations ultérieures n'aient rien trouvé à redire à la partie de clarinette arrangée de l'édition usuelle du K.622, jusqu'à ce que la tendance au retour vers les instruments « d'époque » des années 1980 remette inévitablement la question en avant. Hélas, le manuscrit original de Mozart avait alors disparu depuis longtemps et, avec lui, tout manuscrit de la partie séparée utilisée par Stadler pour l'exécution de 1791. Pour Constanze Mozart, la faute en revenait sans aucun doute à Stadler qu'elle accusa d'avoir gagé ce manuscrit, avec plusieurs autres de Mozart, pour 73 pauvres ducats. En revanche, l'esquisse manuscrite du concerto pour cor de basset en *sol* majeur a survécu et fournit plusieurs indices déterminants sur les divergences qui ont pu distinguer la partie de soliste originale de la version entérinée par la tradition. Ainsi, par exemple, des valeurs des mesures 94-95 du premier mouvement : sachant que la clarinette pour laquelle a écrit Mozart pouvait atteindre le *do* grave (noté), l'instabilité du mouvement à partir des trois dernières croches de la mesure 94 jusqu'aux doubles croches de la mesure 95 saute littéralement aux yeux. Même en se passant du témoignage du brouillon original pour cor de basset, la simple analogie avec les mesures 96-97 suffirait à montrer ce qu'étaient sûrement les intentions initiales de Mozart. Il est difficile de croire que Mozart, même sous le coup d'une pression intense, ait choisi une transposition aussi partielle et brusque que celle perpétuée depuis la première édition. Un autre exemple frappant est constitué par l'apogée de l'*Adagio* (mesures 55 *et seq.*). Avec un instrument possédant une tierce majeure supplémentaire dans le registre inférieur, tel que celui de Stadler, il n'y avait pas besoin d'interrompre les arpèges de doubles croches sur le deuxième temps des mesures 55 et 57. Un mouvement ascendant continu à partir du *do* grave, plus élégant, permettait au soliste de déployer un éventail beaucoup plus large de coloration sonore à cet endroit crucial et dramatique du mouvement.

L'intérêt pour l'original du Concerto pour clarinette s'étant éveillé récemment, des tentatives de reconstitution de la partie de soliste conformément aux intentions supposées de Mozart ont vu le jour, ainsi que la reconstruction d'une clarinette disposant de la même tessiture de basse que l'instrument de Stadler et appelée

« clarinette de basset ». Cet instrument, qui s'est progressivement imposé au concert et dans les studios d'enregistrement, jouit désormais d'une popularité presqu'égale à celle de la clarinette en *la* moderne, sans que celle-ci ne montre aucun signe de déclin sérieux pour l'interprétation du K.622.

Le fait que le Concerto pour clarinette soit la dernière grande œuvre achevée de Mozart a inévitablement, à juste titre ou non, influé sur la manière dont il a été interprété et analysé. Le spécialiste de Mozart, H. C. Robbins Landon, ne s'attendait pas à être sérieusement contredit quand il écrivit : « aucune autre œuvre de Mozart n'est plus imprégnée de cette résignation ultime et sereine […] Le concerto représente l'adieu de Mozart au règne de la musique pure. »[2] Robbins Landon affirme ensuite « En octobre, [Mozart] devait avoir deviné la gravité de sa maladie », mais aucune preuve solide n'étaie cette hypothèse, ni l'idée que Mozart eût une quelconque intuition de sa fin précoce. Lorsque Robbins Landon se repencha sur le sujet, trois décennies plus tard, dans son importante monographie *1791 : Mozart's Last Year*, il révisa substantiellement sa position et avança, au contraire, que Mozart se trouvait à l'aube d'une « ère nouvelle »[3], instiguée par l'immense succès récent de son opéra *Die Zauberflöte*, K.620, et par son impatience à occuper le poste de Kapellmeister à la Cathédrale Saint-Etienne de Vienne qui lui était promis à la mort ou à la retraite de son titulaire Leopold Hofman. Certes, certains passages du Concerto pour clarinette – en particulier dans l'*Adagio* central – se distinguent par la mélancolie de leur expression. On note, de plus, que l'exécution à la clarinette de basset, avec l'extension convenable vers le grave, apporte une coloration généralement plus sombre aux autres passages. Néanmoins, il serait tout aussi facile de reconnaître une « résignation ultime et sereine » dans le mouvement lent et l'introduction du *finale* du Quatuor à cordes en *sol* mineur, K.516, écrit quatre années auparavant. La charge émotionnelle habitant ces deux œuvres s'inscrivait peut-être plutôt dans une possible disposition de caractère dépressif de Mozart que dans une intuition mystique supposée, en octobre 1791, de sa fin prochaine.

Toutefois, le statut mythique conféré au Concerto pour clarinette d'« adieu au règne de la musique pure » s'est prouvé durable et influent. Cette aura presque sacrée dont bénéficie cette œuvre explique peut-être le fait troublant que si peu de concertos marquants pour cet instrument aient été composés depuis la mort de Mozart, en dépit des éminentes qualités de la clarinette comme soliste virtuose pouvant remplir les salles de concert. Le répertoire moderne est, en effet, significativement plus riche en musique de chambre avec clarinette solo qu'en grands concertos pour clarinette et orchestre. De plus, les œuvres les plus importantes pour clarinette et orchestre, depuis les concertos de Weber et de Bernhard Henrik Crusell à celui de Birtwistle *Melencolia I*, n'affichent que de rares traits les rattachant au modèle du Concerto de Mozart. Le mouvement initial du Concerto pour clarinette d'Aaron Copland (1947/48) fait figure d'exception par son ton doucement nostalgique et son utilisation lyrique de larges sauts d'intervalles dans lesquels on peut relever l'influence de Mozart. Toutefois, l'invocation la plus directe de l'œuvre de Mozart se trouve vers la fin du Concerto pour clarinette en un mouvement de Carl Nielsen (1928), datant d'une époque où son compositeur était hanté par la notion de sa propre mortalité. Au repère 41 (*Poco adagio*) du concerto de Nielsen, la clarinette (aussi en *la*) reprend une idée mélodique fondée sur les deux notes (*sol* et *do* réels) qui débutent l'exposition du soliste dans le concerto de Mozart – idée qui se justifierait plus que tout autre du K.622 comme expression de la « résignation ultime et sereine ». S'il s'agit là d'un hommage direct au Concerto pour clarinette de Mozart, sa nature-même, à savoir l'offrande d'un compositeur au seuil de la mort à un autre, explique peut-être la relative rareté de tels hommages.

Stephen Johnson
Traduction : Agnès Ausseur

---

[2] « The Concertos (2) » in :*The Mozart Companion*, éd. H. C. Robbins Landon & Donald Mitchell, Londres, 1956, p.279
[3] H. C. Robbins Landon, *1791: Mozart's Last Year*, Londres, 1988, p.147

CLARINET CONCERTO

Wolfgang Amadeus Mozart
(1756–1791)
K622

I. Allegro

2

4

6

8

10

13

EE 7134

16

18

19

EE 7134

22

24

28

32

34

37

EE 7134

II. Adagio

42

46

III. Rondo
Allegro

47

EE 7134

48

50

52

53

EE 7134

54

55

EE 7134

58

62

70